Spotlight on the
MAYA, AZTEC, and INCA CIVILIZATIONS

# Ancient MAYA DAILY LIFE

Heather Moore Niver

**PowerKiDS** press™

NEW YORK

Published in 2017 by The Rosen Publishing Group, Inc.
29 East 21st Street, New York, NY 10010

Editor: Caitlin McAneney
Book Design: Mickey Harmon

Photo Credits: Cover H. Tom Hall/Contributor/National Geographic/Getty Images; p.5 KKulikov/Shutterstock.com; p. 6 (inset) https://upload.wikimedia.org/wikipedia/commons/0/05/God_G_Kinich_Ahau_2.jpg; p. 6 (main) photograph by Pete Schnell/Moment Open/Getty Images; p. 7 Jad Davenport/National Geographic/Getty Images; pp. 8, 14, 16 Werner Forman/Contributor/Getty Images; p. 9 https://upload.wikimedia.org/wikipedia/commons/8/85/Maya_Codex-Style_Vessel_with_two_scenes_3_Kimbell.jpg; p. 11 DEA/G. DAGLI ORTI/Contributor/Getty Images; p. 12 Terry W. Rutledge/Contributor/National Geographic/Getty Images; p. 13 Universal History Archive/Contributor/Getty Images; p. 15 Ezume Images/Shutterstock.com; p. 17 (illustration) https://upload.wikimedia.org/wikipedia/en/b/bc/Maya_cranial_deformation.gif; p. 17 (skull) https://en.wikipedia.org/wiki/Artificial_cranial_deformation#/media/File:Mayancranialmodification.jpg; pp. 18–19 Peter E. Spier/Contributor/National Geographic/Getty Images; p. 20 MyLoupe/Contributor/Getty Images; p. 21 DEA/W. BUSS/Contributor/Getty Images; p. 23 Danita Delimont/Gallo Images/Getty Images; p. 24 Buda Mendes/Staff/Getty Images Sport/Getty Images; p. 25 https://upload.wikimedia.org/wikipedia/commons/5/5c/Maya_standing_male_warrior%2C_Jaina%2C_c._550-950_C.E.%2C_long-term_loan_to_the_Dayton_Art_Institute.JPG; p. 27 Wolfgang Kaehler/Contributor/Getty Images; p. 29 https://en.wikipedia.org/wiki/Dresden_Codex#/media/File:Dresden_codex,_page_2.jpg

Library of Congress Cataloging-in-Publication Data

Names: Niver, Heather Moore, author.
Title: Ancient Maya daily life / Heather Moore Niver.
Description: New York : PowerKids Press, 2016. | Series: Spotlight on the
  Maya, Aztec, and Inca civilizations | Includes index.
Identifiers: LCCN 2016000866 | ISBN 9781499419634 (pbk.) | ISBN 9781508149026 (library bound) | ISBN 9781499419641 (6 pack)
Subjects: LCSH: Mayas--Juvenile literature.
Classification: LCC F1435 .N59 2016 | DDC 972.81--dc23
LC record available at http://lccn.loc.gov/2016000866

CPSIA Compliance Information: Batch #BS16PK: For further information contact Rosen Publishing, New York, New York at 1-800-237-9932.

# CONTENTS DISCARD

# MEET THE MAYA

The ancient Maya lived in settlements as early as 1800 BC. Their most successful period was from AD 250 to 900. The Maya civilization stretched over areas located in today's Guatemala, Mexico, Belize, Honduras, and El Salvador. The Maya were concentrated in one general area, which often protected them from invasion from other Mesoamerican groups. For many centuries, their civilization was made up of **city-states**, each with its own king.

The daily lives of the Maya were full of many activities, including creating pottery, architecture, and artwork. Many commoners spent their days farming. The Maya used **hieroglyphics** to record events and discoveries. They created a calendar system and made many discoveries in mathematics, astronomy, and science. Curiously, the Maya deserted many of their cities around AD 900. Many details of the Maya civilization remain a mystery, but historians use **artifacts** and ruins to better understand their daily life.

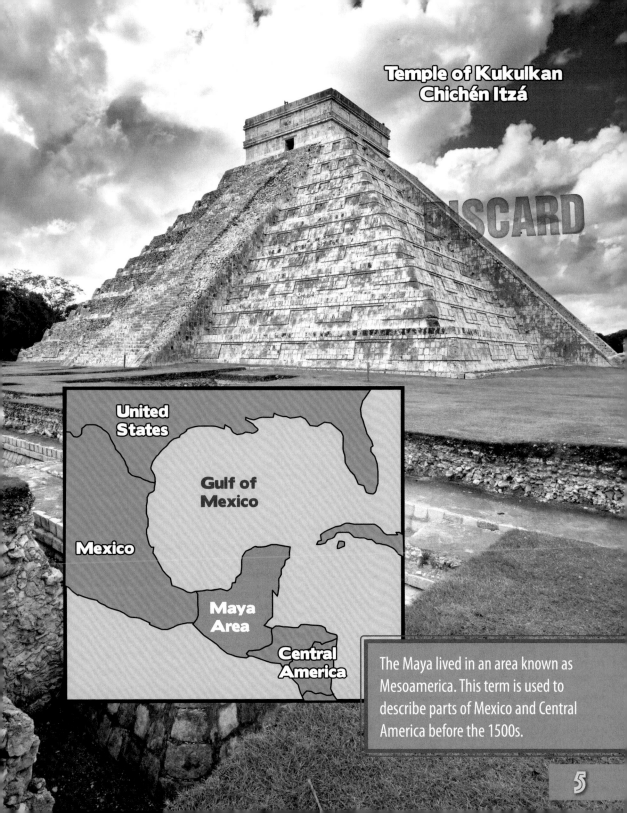

**Temple of Kukulkan Chichén Itzá**

United States

Gulf of Mexico

Mexico

Maya Area

Central America

The Maya lived in an area known as Mesoamerica. This term is used to describe parts of Mexico and Central America before the 1500s.

# KINGS AND NOBLES

Many ancient societies were based on class, and the Maya were no different. Their daily lives centered on class structure. At the top were kings and nobles. The noble class usually included the best warriors, as well as priests, scribes, and government officials. The nobility was the smallest of all the classes, but it had the most power and the most wealth.

KINICH AHAU

Kings and nobles usually lived in the city-state center, but smaller villages, like the one shown here, existed outside the center.

This is the palace of Palenque in today's state of Chiapas, Mexico, where the kings of the city-state would have spent their days.

The Maya believed that nobles were go-betweens for people and their gods. Kings were responsible to gods, and nobles were responsible to both gods and people. The kings governed and got advice from a council of nobles. In cities like Palenque, the king's name started with *kinich*, a title that meant "great sun." The Maya believed these kings were related to the sun god, Kinich Ahau.

Kings and nobles often lived in large, highly decorated palaces that showed their wealth. However, other nobles lived in smaller, wooden homes.

# MAYA PRIESTS

Priests were an important part of Maya life. They were almost as powerful as kings. They were in charge of performing religious ceremonies and rituals and teaching young Maya nobles. They studied and made discoveries in the fields of math, astronomy, and astrology and then taught others what they knew. Priests had many roles in daily Maya life. They were in charge of keeping the calendars. They kept track of family history. Sometimes they even told people about what might happen in the future.

Sometimes priests went without food for a long time

This figurine might represent a Maya priest.

This ancient Maya vessel shows a scene between a Maya god and a keeper of holy books, who is possibly a priest.

as part of their rituals. Some of the rituals they performed were painful. They pierced their skin with thorns and offered their blood to their gods. Priests did these things because they thought such acts helped them communicate with their gods. Maya priests performed religious ceremonies often because they had so many gods.

# THE LIFE OF A COMMONER

Other Maya people worked as artisans, traders, potters, soldiers, and farmers. They were also called commoners. Agriculture was important to Maya life. Farmers and laborers tended to the fields, which provided enough food to eat and trade. Most Maya commoners worked as farmers during the growing season. Once the crops were **harvested**, people often helped build the Maya's magnificent cities. Each day included hard physical work for the benefit of their society.

Commoner women created **textiles** and artwork, many of which were very colorful and decorative. They also helped farm crops and herd animals. They cooked, cared for gardens, and raised children. Their work was a big help to the economy. Most of the time women didn't have a part in politics. However, as Maya society grew, their politics became more **complex**, and some women became queens.

This figurine represents a Maya woman weaving.

# WHO WERE ARTISANS?

Artisans worked at creating things. They were considered commoners, but their lives were a little easier than those of the farmers. The Maya were well known for their beautiful crafts. Their artisans created jewelry, textiles, pottery, and **accessories** such as feather wraps and headdresses. Some Maya art, such as jewelry and stonework, still exists today.

Artisans usually lived in one-room homes with their **nuclear families** or extended families. Besides parents and children, there might be aunts, uncles, and grandparents all under one roof.

This artwork shows a Maya artisan displaying his pottery.

Some Maya artisans spent their days making jewelry, such as this set made of jade.

The artisans likely started their day early. Breakfast was often *saka*, which was made of cornmeal combined with water. It was usually given extra flavor with chilis or honey. Wealthy artisans might enjoy a cup of hot chocolate. Artisans might go to the marketplace for supplies and materials, or go to work in a type of studio. After work, the family would gather for a big meal.

# DAILY LIFE OF FARMERS

Maya farmers also started their days very early. Families slept together in a single-room house. Everyone slept on mats made from reeds. They began their day with a simple breakfast of *saka*, much like the artisans.

After their bellies were full, farmers and farmhands headed out to work in the fields. They usually wore

Most Maya commoners lived together in a one-room house, like this one.

Maize, or corn, was an important part of the Maya diet. Descendants of the ancient Maya still use it in many of their meals.

**loincloths**. If it was a cold day, they would also wear a cape. They took a midday meal with them. It was usually a dumpling made of cornmeal dough and filled with vegetables and meat. The women went to work, too. Some were weavers, while others also went to the fields to work.

When the day's work was done, the family met back at the house. They ate their main meal together. They filled tortillas with vegetables, and meat or fish if those foods were available. Once the sun set and night fell, everyone went to sleep.

# BODY MODIFICATIONS

The Maya modified, or changed, their bodies in many ways. They filed their teeth to change the shape and decorated them with a green stone called jade. They often pierced their bodies and had many tattoos. Both men and women of all classes got tattoos.

The process of getting a tattoo was painful. First, the tattoo artist painted an image on the skin. Then, they cut the design with a sharp tool. The cut turned into a scar, and along with the paint, it created a tattoo. Tattoos included their gods' symbols or powerful animals, such as snakes, jaguars, or eagles.

This relief, or raised, carving shows a Maya king named Lord Shield Jaguar with a long skull, many accessories, and piercings.

This is an ancient Maya skull, which shows a longer, modified shape.

Babies were modified, too. Mayas would press the baby's soft skull between two pieces of wood so it would grow to have a longer shape. Many body modifications were made to satisfy Maya gods. More modifications meant a higher social rank. Nobles made as many modifications to their bodies as they could.

# VILLAGE TO CITY

At first, all Maya lived in villages. It wasn't until later that they started building city-states. Every city-state was independent, which meant it was in charge of its own government, religion, and economy. Tikal became one of the largest Maya city-states. It may have stretched over an area of more than 6 square miles (15.5 sq km). It was made up of nearly 3,000 buildings and had more than 60,000 people living there. Other important Maya cities included Calakmul, Palenque, and Copán, which are located in what

is now Mexico and Honduras. The Mayas built 40 city-states between AD 250 and AD 900, which was the peak of their civilization.

Each Maya city was different because they were built to work best with their surroundings. Many had stepped pyramids, temples, palaces, and monuments carved out of stone. Although the cities had different designs, most were built around a main plaza, or open public area.

The Maya city of Tikal was one of the largest of all the city-states.

# HOUSES AND BUILDINGS

The Maya built temples around the central plazas of their cities. They also constructed palaces, courts for playing ball, and homes for the **elite**. Smaller plazas were built beyond the city center and were surrounded by commoners' homes. The Maya used stone walkways to connect the central plaza to the places where commoners lived.

These are the ruins of the Great Plaza in the ancient Maya city of Tikal.

This is the central plaza of the ancient city-state of Edzná.

A city's main buildings were huge and made out of stone. Many were constructed using **limestone**. Stoneworkers cut large blocks of limestone with tools also made out of stone. Limestone is soft but it hardens after it's cut out of the ground.

Most Maya commoners lived in houses they built using materials from nearby rain forests, such as wood and vines. The houses were rectangular with rounded corners. Some people slept in hammocks inside their huts during the rainy season. The Maya cooked some of their food in pits outside their huts, but there were also places to cook inside.

# WHAT DID THE MAYA EAT?

The Maya ate a wide variety of foods, including peppers, beans, and squash. They also grew a root called cassava, or manioc. Corn—also called maize—was their main crop, which they used in nearly every meal. They ate fruits such as avocados, papayas, and guavas. The Maya usually ate what they grew, but sometimes they traded with other groups. They traded vanilla and **cacao** beans.

The ancient Maya appear to have used several methods of farming. They used a slash-and-burn method, which involved several steps. First, they cut down trees in an area, and then they burned them there. Finally, they planted their crops in the rich, ashy soil. The Maya also used raised beds made out of mud and reed mats to keep their crops dry in swampy areas. On mountainsides, they built terraces—or flat areas for farming—into the slope. Some Maya women raised herds of deer, which provided meat for their villages or city-states.

The ancient Maya had a god of chocolate and a god of corn, which shows how important those crops were to their daily life. This figurine shows a woman holding a cup of cocoa.

# HUNTING AND WAR

   Hunting was a big part of ancient Maya daily life. The Maya hunted birds, such as quails, turkeys, and ducks. They also hunted the armored armadillo and a large, piglike animal called a tapir. Monkeys and even dogs were sometimes sources of food. The Maya had many weapons for hunting. Blowguns were weapons used for both hunting and fighting during war.

This Brazilian tribesman demonstrates the use of a blowgun similar to those used by the ancient Maya.

Historians once believed the Maya were generally peaceful, but they've discovered the Maya went to war often. They especially fought many wars between AD 600 and AD 900. This is probably because times were tough for the Maya. There's evidence that they suffered from overpopulation, which led to a shortage of food. There also may have been a drought, or a long period of little rain. Their slash-and-burn farming may have destroyed the soil. They went to war for more food to feed their people. City-states also fought over power, boundaries, and prisoners captured for sacrifice.

This figurine shows a Maya warrior, ready for battle.

# RELIGION AND RITUALS

The Maya's daily life included practicing a complex religious system. The Maya worshipped more than 150 gods! Their supreme, or highest, god was most likely called Itzamna. Itzamna was the god of science and writing. The sun god Kinich Ahau may have been an individual god, or he may have been a part of Itzamna.

Kings and priests were responsible for overseeing and performing the Maya religious ceremonies. Women didn't usually have a part in this, but there may have been priestesses in later Maya society.

The Maya were accomplished astronomers. They built circle-shaped buildings for watching the skies and studying stars and planets. Their investigation of the sky led to the creation of their own calendar. The Maya also played a game with a ball that might have represented the sun's orbit around Earth.

These are the ruins of a Maya observatory on Mexico's Yucatán Peninsula.

# KEEPING TRACK OF THEIR DAYS

The lives of the ancient Maya were full of activities, including work, family meals, and religious rituals and events. The Maya kept track of time through natural cycles, such as the corn's growing season. Sometimes they offered corn to their gods at the end of a growing season. This offering marked the beginning of a new season.

The Maya also kept track of their days with calendars, which were based on math and astronomy. They were very good at using science and math to develop technology. Scientists today realize that Maya calendars were very accurate. The Maya had a religious calendar and a calendar based on the sun. Their ideas of time were based around movement of the sun and the moon across the sky, and the growing season. The Maya calendar system and their complex culture show how advanced this civilization became, one day at a time.

The Dresden Codex is the best source of information about Maya calendar systems and astronomy. It shows tables for religious ceremony schedules and future events based on the motions of the sun and moon.

# LEAVING THEIR CITIES

For some reason, around the year AD 900, the Maya left many of their great cities and returned to village life. Their civilization fell very quickly. Some historians think drought and war might have been the major causes. Wars might have caused a change in their trade routes.

Some cities in the north—such as Chichén Itzá, Uxmal, and Mayapán—continued to do well until the Spanish invaded. By 1546, most of the Maya cities in the northern Yucatán peninsula were under Spanish control. Many Maya became slaves to the Spanish, and many died from new diseases the Spanish brought.

Today, around 6 million Maya still live in Mexico and Central America, in countries including Guatemala and Belize. Many still farm like their ancestors did. They still make pottery and weave traditional patterns into their native clothing. By doing so, many modern Maya try to **incorporate** their heritage into their daily lives.

# GLOSSARY

**accessory (aak-SEH-suh-ree):** Something added to something else to make it more attractive or decorated.

**artifact (AAR-tih-fact):** Something made by humans in the past.

**cacao (keh-KAY-oh):** Seeds from the cacao tree that are used to make cocoa, chocolate, and cocoa butter.

**city-state (SIH-tee–STAYT):** An independent city and the land around it.

**complex (kahm-PLEHKS):** Made up of different parts, sometimes not easy to understand.

**elite (eh-LEET):** The people in a society who are thought to be the greatest.

**harvest (HAR-vehst):** To collect crops from the fields when they are ready and ripe.

**hieroglyphics (hy-roh-GLIH-fihks):** An ancient form of writing made of small images.

**incorporate (ihn-KOHR-puh-rayt):** To combine something with something else.

**limestone (LYM-stohn):** A stone used to create buildings.

**loincloth (LOYN-cloth):** One length of cloth wrapped around the hips, usually worn by men.

**nuclear family (NEW-clee-uhr FAM-lee):** The part of a family that includes a mother, father, and their children.

**textile (TEHK-styl):** A kind of cloth or fabric, sometimes made by weaving.

# INDEX

# PRIMARY SOURCE LIST

**Page 9:** Codex-Style Vessel with Two Scenes of Pawahtun Instructing Scribes. Ceramic with monochrome decoration. Possibly Mexico or Guatemala. Late Classic Period (AD 600 to 900). Now kept at the Kimbell Art Museum, Fort Worth, Texas.

**Page 16:** Detail from Lintel 26 from Structure 23 at Yaxchilan. Relief carving in limestone. Yaxchilan, State of Chiapas, Mexico. Late Classic Period (AD 600 to 900). Now kept at the National Museum of Anthropology, Mexico City, Mexico.

**Page 29:** Dresden Codex, page 49. Possibly created in or near Chichén Itzá, Yucatán, Mexico. Circa AD 1200 to 1250. Now kept at Saxon State and University Library Dresden, Dresden, Germany.

# WEBSITES

Due to the changing nature of Internet links, PowerKids Press has developed an online list of websites related to the subject of this book. This site is updated regularly. Please use this link to access the list: www.powerkidslinks.com/soac/mayadl